the best of grades 1–3
Singing
Low voice

Selected and edited by Heidi Pegler

FABER *ff* MUSIC

© 2012 by Faber Music Ltd
This edition first published in 2012
Bloomsbury House
74–77 Great Russell Street
London WC1B 3DA
Music processed by Jackie Leigh
Design by Økvik Design
Printed in England by Caligraving Ltd
All rights reserved

ISBN10: 0-571-53684-0
EAN13: 978-0-571-53684-9

To buy Faber Music publications or to find out about the full range of titles available
please contact your local music retailer or Faber Music sales enquiries:

Faber Music Limited, Burnt Mill, Elizabeth Way, Harlow CM20 2HX
Tel: +44 (0)1279 82 89 82   Fax: +44 (0)1279 82 89 83
sales@fabermusic.com   fabermusicstore.com

Audio tracks produced by Andrew McKenna Music

Contents

My grandfather's clock

ACCOMPANIMENT

This song was reputedly inspired by the story of a longcase clock that ticked steadily for years
and years, but finally stopped when its owners died. Keep in strict time, observing the rests
and singing with crisp, clear words.

H. C. Work
arr. Heidi Pegler

Bugeilio'r Gwenith Gwyn (Watching the Wheat)

ACCOMPANIMENT

This well-known Welsh folksong allegedly describes a young man's love for the rich heiress Ann Thomas – the so-called 'Maid of Cefn Ydfa'. Ann reportedly died of a broken heart after being forced to marry another man against her will.

Trad. Welsh
arr. Heidi Pegler

Lavender's blue

ACCOMPANIMENT ③

'Lavender's blue' is an English folksong dating from about the seventeenth century and has been passed down through generations. Make sure the interval jumps are accurate and the descending scales stay in tune – don't go flat!

Trad. English
arr. Heidi Pegler

1. La - ven - der's blue, dil - ly, dil - ly, la - ven - der's green.
2. Call up your men, dil - ly, dil - ly, set them to work,

When I am king, dil - ly, dil - ly, you shall be queen.
Some with a rake, dil - ly, dil - ly, some with a fork.

Who told you so, dil - ly, dil - ly? Who told you so?
Some to make hay, dil - ly, dil - ly, some to cut corn,

'Twas my own heart, dil - ly, dil - ly, that told me so.
While you and I, dil - ly, dil - ly, keep our - selves warm.

Orange and Yellow and Brown

ACCOMPANIMENT 4

This wistful song has a catchy tune. Make sure there are no aspirate 'h's in the words 'falling' and 'calling' and ensure you have enough breath and energy to sustain the long tied note in bars 21–2.

Lin Marsh

Seagull

ACCOMPANIMENT 5

The melody line sweeps and soars and perfectly captures the flight of the seagull. Try to depict the wonder and amazement of the bird's journey with engaging facial expression.

Lin Marsh

Marienwürmchen (Ladybird)

No.13 from *Volks-Kinderlieder* WoO 31

ACCOMPANIMENT ⑥

This is a song with a simple melody but a dramatic and well-known story. There is much scope
for expression and drama, particularly in verse 2 with the wicked spider!

Johannes Brahms

English singing translation by Heidi Pegler

We're off to see the Wizard

from *The Wizard Of Oz*

This is a classic song which is fun to sing and will appeal to all ages. A really good performance will need light and energetic singing with crisp, clear words.

ACCOMPANIMENT

Music by Harold Arlen
Lyrics by E. Y. Harburg

It's a lovely day today

from *Call Me Madam*

ACCOMPANIMENT 8

This song has an optimistic and happy melody which is bound to go down well in a performance. Make sure you practise the interval jumps in the last five bars – these need to be spot on!

Words and Music by
Irving Berlin

After the ball

This lively waltz was a very popular song in the 1890s and has sold over 5 million copies. Try to hold the long notes for their full duration and follow the dynamics to shape the phrases musically.

Words and Music by
Charles K. Harris

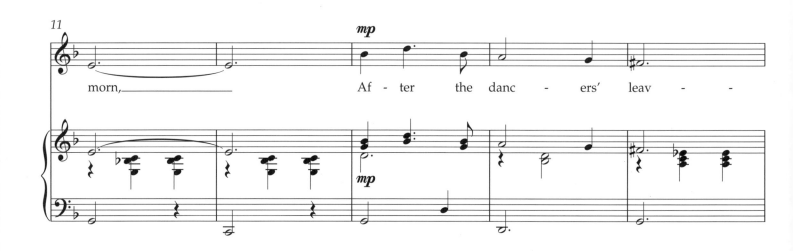

Let's Go Fly a Kite

from *Mary Poppins*

ACCOMPANIMENT

When George Banks finally realises that his family is more important than his job, he mends his son's kite and takes his family on a kite-flying outing. This is a song full of optimism and should be sung with gusto!

Words and Music by
Richard M. Sherman and Robert B. Sherman

Cockles and Mussels

There is a statue of Molly Malone in Dublin, although it is widely thought that she is a fictional character. This song is a good choice if you like telling a story as there is a lot of scope for characterisation and expression.

Trad. Irish
arr. Pam Wedgwood

1. In Dublin's fair city, where girls are so pretty, I first set my eyes on sweet Molly Malone, As she wheeled her wheel-barrow through streets broad and narrow, Crying, 'Cockles and mussels! A-live, a-live oh!' 'A-live, a-live oh!' A-live, a-live

Let him go, let him tarry

ACCOMPANIMENT 12

Here is a song with attitude which needs to be sung in a confident manner. Practise the interval leaps in bar 3 as this tonic triad occurs throughout the song and needs to be secure and on pitch.

Trad. Irish
arr. Heidi Pegler

1. Fare-well   to cold Win - ter
2. He wrote me a   let - ter say-ing

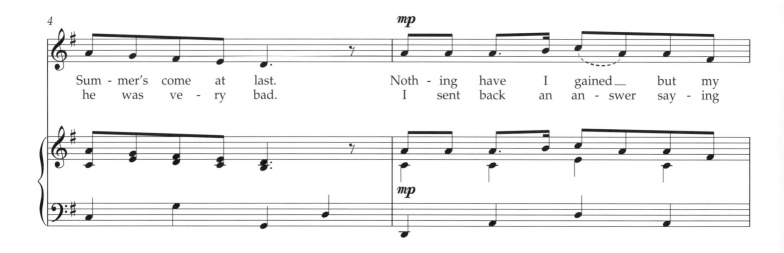

Sum - mer's come   at   last.   Noth - ing   have   I   gained___ but   my
he was ve - ry   bad.   I   sent   back   an an - swer say - ing

true   love   I   have   lost.   I'll   sing   and   I'll   be   hap - py   like   the
I   was   aw - ful   glad.   He   wrote   to   me   an - oth - er   say - ing

Ma Bella Bimba (How beautiful the ballerina)

ACCOMPANIMENT 13

This lively song requires some energy to sing and it is well worth having a go at the Italian.
Here are some pronunciation points: 'come' – the 'c' is hard, as in *come*; 'che' – *keh* ; 'agile' –
with a soft 'g', as in *geometric*; 'guarda' – *gooahda*.

Trad. Italian
arr. Heidi Pegler

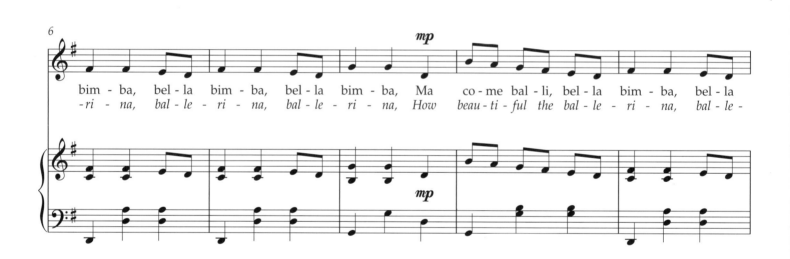

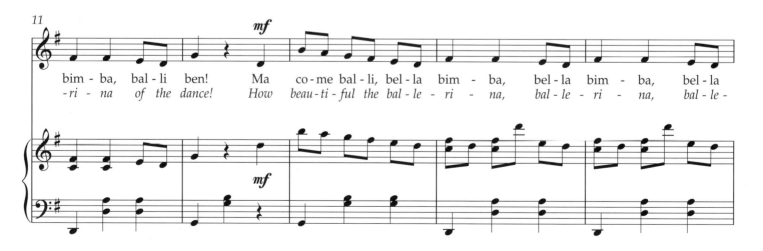

Earth, Sea and Sky

The words are very important in this song and will need careful articulation, particularly at the
start of each verse. Take your time over the triplets in bar 18 and make sure all dotted minims
are held with strength and importance.

Lin Marsh

Wiegenlied (Lullaby)

ACCOMPANIMENT [15]

Op. 98 No. 2, D. 498

In this lovely song, imagine the piano part as the gentle rocking of the cradle, but be careful not
to go too slowly. Try adding some suitable dynamic changes in each verse to match the rise
and fall of the tune and words.

Franz Schubert

English singing translation by Heidi Pegler

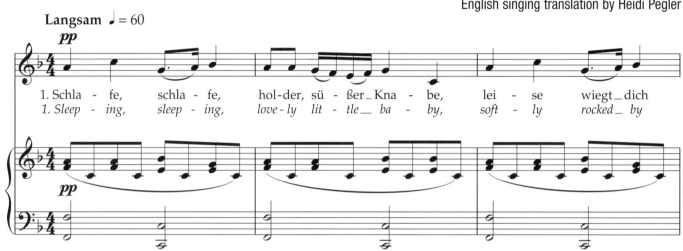

2. Schla - fe, schla - fe, in dem sü - ßen Gra - be, noch be - schützt dich
2. Sleep - ing, sleep - ing, in your rock - ing cra - dle, loved and shel - tered
3. Schla - fe, schla - fe, in der Flau - men Scho - ße, noch um - tönt dich
3. Sleep - ing, sleep - ing, on your dow - ny pil - low, songs and lul - la - bies

dei - ner Mut - ter Arm; al - le Wün - sche, al - le Ha - be faßt sie lie - bend,
by your mo - ther's arm; all her wish - es, all her pos - ses - sions she will use to
lau - ter Lie - bes - ton, ei - ne Li - lie, ei - ne Ro - se, nach dem Schla - fe
float - ing through the air, all the li - lies, all the ro - ses, af - ter sleep will

al - le lie - be - warm.
keep you safe and warm.
werd sie dir zum Lohn.
wait to greet you there.

Sans Day Carol

ACCOMPANIMENT 16

The 'Sans Day Carol' (or 'St. Day Carol') is a Cornish Christmas carol from the nineteenth century. Make sure there is a difference between the ♩. ♪ pattern (bars 4–5) and the ♪ ♩ (bars 8–9).

Trad.
arr. Heidi Pegler

1. Now   the
2. Now   the

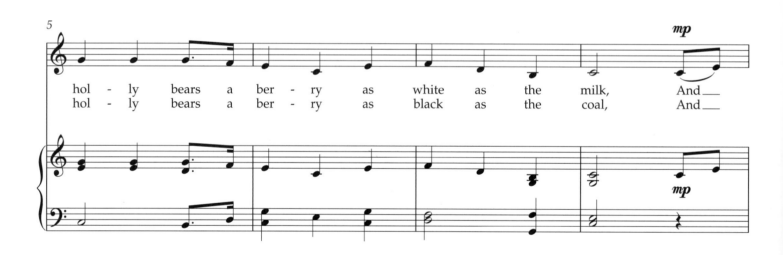

hol - ly   bears   a   ber - ry   as   white   as   the   milk,   And___
hol - ly   bears   a   ber - ry   as   black   as   the   coal,   And___

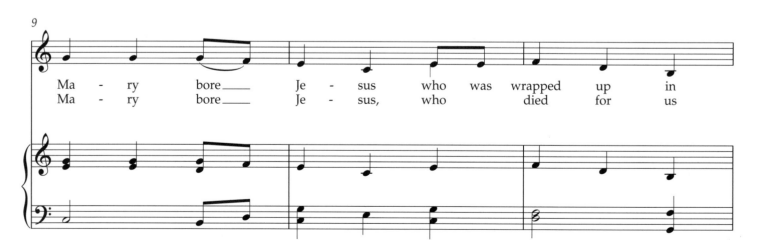

Ma - ry   bore___   Je - sus   who   was   wrapped   up   in
Ma - ry   bore___   Je - sus,   who   died   for   us

Singin' in the Rain

from *Singin' In The Rain*

ACCOMPANIMENT [17]

This song is the centre piece of the musical film *Singin' In The Rain* (1952), which Gene Kelly danced to while splashing through puddles. Make sure the tuning of the octave jumps is really accurate to sound convincing and secure.

Music by Nacio Herb Brown
Lyrics by Arthur Freed

Flash, Bang, Wallop!

This song describes taking a wedding photograph at the turn of the twentieth century before
the invention of digital cameras. It is a tongue-twister in places but is great fun to sing and you
could even add some body percussion in the chorus!

Words and Music by
David Heneker

14

in his fur Took a trip up to Gret - na Green, There's al - ways been a pho-
birth - day suit, De - cid - ed to get wed, As Ad - am was a - bout to

18   *rit.*   **a tempo**

-to - graph - er To re - cord the hap - py scene.
taste the fruit, The man with the cam - 'ra said:

21 *mf*

Hold it, flash, bang, wal - lop, what a pic - ture, Click, what a pic - ture,

24

What a pho - to - graph.
1. Poor old soul,   Bli - mey, what a joke,
2. Poor old Eve –   There with noth - ing on,

Hat blown off in a cloud of smoke. Clap hands!
Face all red and her fig leaf gone. Clap hands!

Stamp your feet!__ Bang it on the big bass drum. What a pic - ture,

what a pic - ture. Rum tid-de-ly um pum, pum, pum, pum. Stick it in the fam - 'ly

al - bum!   2. The   al - bum!

Daisy Bell

ACCOMPANIMENT 19

This famous music hall number was inspired by Harry Dacre's trip to the US, when he was
charged custom tax on his bicycle. A friend apparently said: 'It's lucky you didn't bring a bicycle
built for two, otherwise you'd have to pay double duty.'

Harry Dacre
arr. Heidi Pegler

Hushabye Mountain

from *Chitty Chitty Bang Bang*

This song appears first as a peaceful lullaby sung by Caractacus Potts to his children and later
to comfort the children of Vulgaria. This gentle song ebbs and flows throughout to mimic the
breeze and the bobbing boats.

ACCOMPANIMENT 20

Words and Music by
Richard M. Sherman and Robert B. Sherman

Pretty Polly Oliver

ACCOMPANIMENT 21

This English folksong tells the story of a woman who disguises herself as a man in order to follow her lover into the army. There are several characters in this song and it is important to find a different vocal colour for each.

Trad. English
arr. Heidi Pegler

As pret-ty Pol-ly O-li-ver lay mu-sing in bed, A co-mi-cal fan-cy came_ in-to her head: 'Nor fa-ther nor mo-ther_ shall_ make me false prove, I'll list for a sol-dier and fol-low my love.' The

sol - dier here weep - ing,— a— sol - dier a - fraid?' 'Oh, Sir! I'm no

sol - dier,' said Pol - ly, 'I'm a maid.' 'A maid?' said the

Cap - tain, 'Then throw her in jail.' 'Oh no,' plead - ed Pol - ly, who—

told her sad tale, And when a great vic - t'ry— had— end - ed the

strife The Cap - tain took Pol - ly and made— her his wife.

Camptown Races

 ACCOMPANIMENT 22

The phrase 'camp town' refers to makeshift towns in America that were populated by migrant workers and set up around train tracks to make travelling easy. In this song a group of migrants place a bet on horses to try to make some money.

Words and Music by Stephen Foster

arr. Heidi Pegler

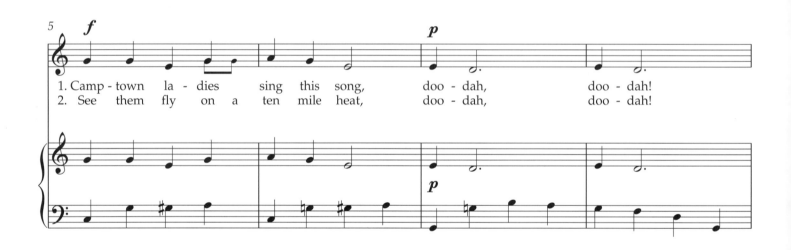

> 1. Camp-town la - dies sing this song, doo - dah, doo - dah!
> 2. See them fly on a ten mile heat, doo - dah, doo - dah!

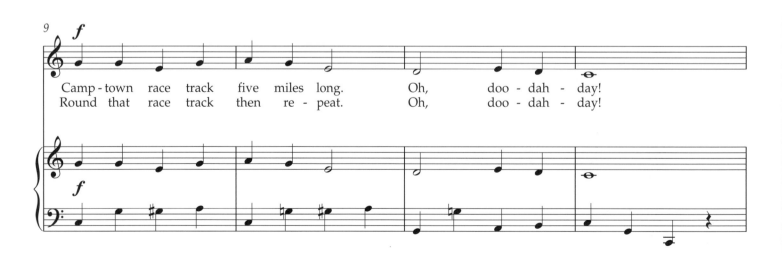

> Camp-town race track five miles long. Oh, doo - dah - day!
> Round that race track then re - peat. Oh, doo - dah - day!

I know where I'm goin'

ACCOMPANIMENT 23

This song closes with the words 'But the dear knows who I'll marry!', meaning 'who knows who I'll marry'. This unfinished business is reflected in the music's unresolved final phrase. Observe the dynamic markings to bring your performance to life.

Trad. Irish
arr. Pam Wedgwood

Fea - ther beds are soft, And paint - ed rooms are bon - ny; But

I would leave them all To__ go with my love John - ny.

Majestically

I know where I'm go - in',__ And I know who's go - in' with me;

I know who I love, But the dear knows who I'll mar - ry!

Butterfly

Try to capture the image of the butterfly flitting and darting about in your performance.
Breathing should be quick and inaudible, and make sure you follow the punctuation marks
throughout. See if you can sing bars 16–19 in one breath!

Lin Marsh

Zwei Braune Augen (Two Brown Eyes)

ACCOMPANIMENT 25

Op. 5 No. 1

This song dances along and is full of love and adoration. Pay attention to the tempo changes in bars 13–15 and demonstrate your sensitivity as a performer by delivering a really soft and tender ending.

Edvard Grieg

English singing translation by Heidi Pegler

The Gower Wassail

ACCOMPANIMENT 26

The Gower is a peninsula in South Wales and a wassail in this case is a hot, mulled punch
made with sugar, cinnamon, ginger, and nutmeg and topped with slices of toast! Sing at a lively
pace and with plenty of character, especially in the *fol-de-dol* choruses.

Trad. Welsh
arr. Heidi Pegler

Chim Chim Cher-ee

ACCOMPANIMENT

from *Mary Poppins*

Tradition has it that it is good luck to shake hands with a chimney sweep and they were often invited to weddings for exactly this purpose! Don't forget that this song requires a Cockney accent in order to capture the character.

Words and Music by
Richard M. Sherman and Robert B. Sherman

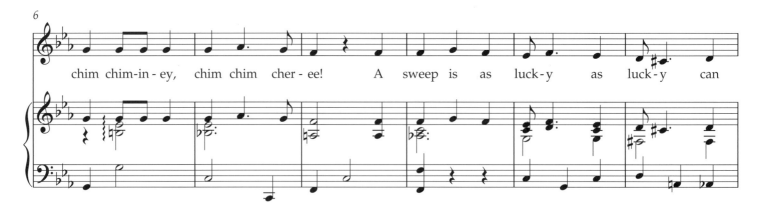

that's luck - y too.   Now, as the
I choose me

lad - der of life 'as been strung, you may think a sweep's on the
bris - tles with pride, yes, I do: a broom for the shaft and a

bot - tom - most rung. Though I spends me time in the ash - es and
brush for the flue. Though I'm cov - ered with soot from me 'ead to me

1.

smoke, in this 'ole wide world there's no 'ap - pi - er bloke.
toes, a sweep knows 'e's wel - come wher - ev - er 'e

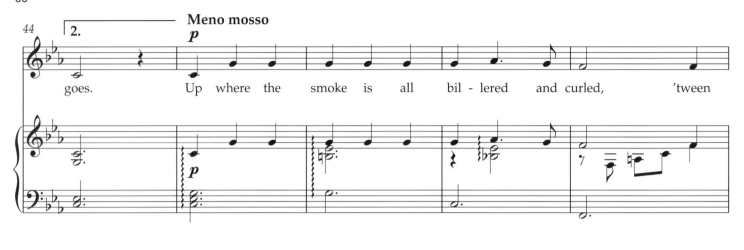

Meno mosso

2.

goes. Up where the smoke is all bil - lered and curled, 'tween

pave - ment and stars, is the chim - ney sweep world. When there's 'ard - ly no

day nor 'ard - ly no night, there's things 'alf in sha-dow and

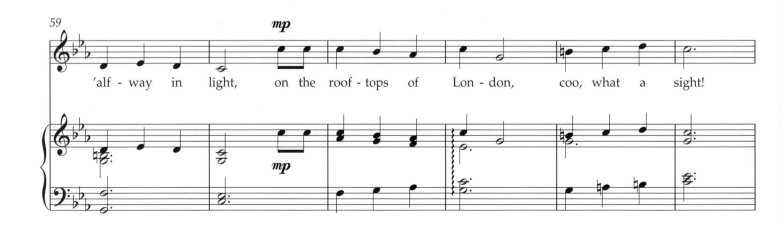

'alf - way in light, on the roof - tops of Lon - don, coo, what a sight!

Tempo I

Chim chim-in-ey, chim chim-in-ey, chim chim cher-ee! When you're with a sweep you're in glad com-pa-ny. No-where is there a more 'ap-pi-er crew than them wot sings, 'Chim chim cher-ee, chim cher-oo!' Chim chim-in-ey, chim chim, cher-ee, chim cher-oo!

The Deadwood Stage

from *Calamity Jane*

ACCOMPANIMENT

This song describes the journey of the local transportation (horse and carriage) from Chicago to Deadwood and all the dangers that it encounters on the way. The words need to be really clear and vibrant with lots of energy and excitement.

Words by Paul Webster
Music by Sammy Fain

Wouldn't it be Loverly?

ACCOMPANIMENT

from *My Fair Lady*

This song is sung by the flower-seller Eliza at the start of *My Fair Lady* as she imagines having
a different kind of life. It needs a Cockney accent to bring out the character as well as lots of
facial expression and word articulation.

Words by Alan Jay Lerner
Music by Frederick Loewe

Let's Face the Music and Dance

ACCOMPANIMENT

This song is great fun to sing, but make sure you learn the notes correctly first as it moves between major and minor! Give the phrases some dynamic shape throughout, and try pronouncing the words 'dance' and 'chance' with a slight American accent to capture the style.

Words and Music by
Irving Berlin

the Language of Song

18 classic Italian, German, French and Spanish songs, with background notes, translations and pronunciation guides

20 classic Italian, German and French songs, with background notes, translations and pronunciation guides

Language of Song: Intermediate
ISBN10: 0-571-52344-7
EAN13: 978-0-571-52344-3

Language of Song: Elementary
ISBN10: 0-571-52346-3
EAN13: 978-0-571-52346-7

Tu lo sai • Giuseppe Torelli
Toglietemi la vita ancor • Alessandro Scarlatti
Amarilli, mia bella . Giulio Caccini
Se tu m'ami • attr. Alessandro Parisotti
Vaga luna • Vincenzo Bellini
An Chloë • Wolfgang Amadeus Mozart
Vergebliches Ständchen • Johannes Brahms
Ständchen • Franz Schubert
Mariä Wiegenlied • Max Reger
Die Lotosblume • Robert Schumann
Die Forelle • Franz Schubert
Le charme • Ernest Chausson
Le secret • Gabriel Fauré
Aurore • Gabriel Fauré
Clair de lune • Gabriel Fauré
El majo discreto • Enrique Granados
En Jerez de la Frontera • Joaquín Rodrigo
Canción de cuna para dormir a un negrito • Xavier Montsalvatge

Caro mio ben • Tommaso Giordani
Santa Lucia • Teodoro Cottrau
Non lo dirò col labbro • Georg Frideric Handel
Sebben, crudele • Antonio Caldara
Nina • Anonymous
Alma del core • Antonio Caldara
Nel cor più non mi sento • Giovanni Paisiello
Vittoria, mio core! • Giacomo Carissimi
Gruß • Felix Mendelssohn
An die Laute • Franz Schubert
Kinderwacht • Robert Schumann
Frühlingslied • Franz Schubert
Wiegenlied • Johannes Brahms
Sonntag • Johannes Brahms
Heidenröslein • Franz Schubert
Dein blaues Aug • Johannes Brahms
Chevaliers de la table ronde • French folksong
Bois épais • Jean-Baptiste Lully
En prière • Gabriel Fauré
Lydia • Gabriel Fauré

To buy Faber Music publications or to find out about the full range of titles available please contact your local music retailer or Faber Music sales enquiries:

Faber Music Ltd, Burnt Mill, Elizabeth Way, Harlow CM20 2HX
Tel: +44 (0) 1279 82 89 82   Fax: +44 (0) 1279 82 89 83
sales@fabermusic.com   fabermusicstore.com

the Language of Song

24 classic Italian, German, French and Russian songs,
with background notes, translations and pronunciation guides

Language of Song: Advanced
ISBN10: 0-571-53077-X
EAN13: 978-0-571-53077-9

FABER ff MUSIC

To buy Faber Music publications or to find out about the full range of titles available
please contact your local music retailer or Faber Music sales enquiries:

Faber Music Ltd, Burnt Mill, Elizabeth Way, Harlow CM20 2HX
Tel: +44 (0) 1279 82 89 82   Fax: +44 (0) 1279 82 89 83
sales@fabermusic.com   fabermusicstore.com